Publisher's Note

A Word From Tony

I0463564

I have been overwhelmed by the enthusiastic response United States General Statues Pamphlets has received since its inception. I am grateful and humbled by the support received from the staff and volunteers who lent their expertise by knocking on doors, making phone calls, sending mail or simply telling a friend.

I also want to thank the public for your overwhelming support which has allowed General Statues Pamphlet Publications to reach and exceed our first publication goals. In the end, the margin of victory was more than I could have ever expected when we started.

I am the executive publisher for Vision Books. We proudly publish the General Statues Pamphlets for the United States of America! These are 5 x 8 soft back pamphlets. No need to purchase the entire legal General Statues book. Just order the chapters that you need to serve your legal needs. Here are some examples:

Example 1): If you are incarcerated and you wanted to know if your trial process was handled in accordance with Civil procedure. You may want to order Pamphlets 1 & 2 which cover Civil Procedure.

Example 2): If you are incarcerated and you want to know about your criminal charges. You may want to order Pamphlet(s) 7,8,9,10 & 11.

Example 3): If you are incarcerated and you want to know about filing Habeas Corpus (How to get back into court?) You may want to order pamphlet 11.

This Publication is only a General Reference Guide. You may use it to purchase the General Statues Pamphlets that will serve your needs. There is an order form in the rear of this Pamphlet, just fill it out and we can bill a third party (mother, father, sister, brother, any relative or friend, etc.) on your behalf. This publication has been pre-paid by a family member, friend or clergy member.

If you do not need any General Statue Pamphlets, please refer this General Reference Guide to other individuals who may need assistance with their individual cases.

The enclosed guide is for the state of North Carolina. However, we publish General Statue Pamphlets for all 50 states. Just select your state from the order form on page 27 and after you receive your General Reference Guide for your state. You will be able to order the pamphlets of your choice.

It has also come to my attention that some pre-paid publications have not been delivered to the addressee. Please see the attached legal note.

We hope that you enjoy this General Reference Guide as much as we enjoyed putting it together. Let us know your thoughts and be sure to come visit us at www.usastatecodes.com or contact customer service at 980.729.3505

Best Wishes,

Tony Rivers Sr.
Executive Publisher

Vision Books
4325 Harris Boulevard, P.O. Box 42406,
Charlotte, NC 28215-1985
Tel. 980.729.3505   Office/Fax. 980.299.5965
Email: staff@visionbooks.com

Attn: General Statues Subscriber;

From the Office of the Publisher & Chief Editor

It has come to my attention that paid and pre-paid subscriptions of General Statues Pamphlets are not being delivered to the addressee. The enclosed copy of the General Reference Guide for the state of North Carolina is being tracked by the United States Postal Service (USPS), Washington, D.C. Division.

Federal Statutes and Regulations Relating to the Privacy and Security of Mail

The Postal Service has a long tradition of protecting both the cover and contents of mail. Mail protections are grounded in the 4th Amendment, federal criminal and civil statutes, postal statutes and regulations, and court decisions.

Title 18 of the U.S. Code (Crimes and Criminal Procedure) contains all federal criminal laws, including those enforced by the Postal Inspection Service. Title 39 (Postal Service) contains federal civil laws relating to the establishment of the Postal Service and its authority. Other relevant laws are also listed below. The major postal regulations protecting mail are contained in the USPS Administrative Support Manual, Domestic Mail Classification Schedule, Domestic Mail Manual, International Mail Manual, and Postal Operations Manual. Below are some of the more significant federal laws and regulations that pertain to the privacy and security of the mail.

It is a direct federal criminal violation of TITLE 18, U.S. Code: CRIMINAL PROCEDURE by any state or federal law enforcement officer, staff officer, corrections officer, prison

official, or any person, affiliate, or party thereto; too in any way, shape, form or any manner attempt to delay, steal, obstruct, or destroy any legal delivery of United States mail (i.e. magazines, legal books, from direct publishers.) These laws cover all 50 states. These laws protect mail delivery to all U.S. Citizens whether said citizens are incarcerated in any federal, state, city, county, or local municipality city jail, prison, halfway house, or any other institution or facility designed to house prisoners.

Section 1114: Protection of officers and employees of the United States
Section 1701: Obstruction of mails generally
Section 1702: Obstruction of correspondence
Section 1703: Delay or destruction of mail or newspapers
Section 1708: Theft or receipt of stolen mail matter generally
Section 1709: Theft of mail matter by officer or employee (of USPS)
Section 1716: Injurious articles as non-mail able
Section 3061: Investigative powers of Postal Service personnel

This is a pre-paid special edition copy of the General Reference Guide for the state of North Carolina. This subscription has been paid in advance by a friend, family member, or clergy. This General Reference Guide is only a guide to purchase North Carolina General Statues Pamphlets. In order to purchase North Carolina General Statues Pamphlets, you must fill out the enclosed order form located in the rear of the General Reference Guide and bill the subscription to any person of your choice (family member, friend, clergy, etc.) Do not remove this document from this magazine. It may only legally be discarded by the addressee, period!

We ask that you the addressee (receiver of this mail) respond in writing to our agency at the herein described address to confirm that you did receive your paid subscription of the General Statues Reference Pamphlet, and or report any violations of this law. The legal staff at Vision Books will immediately report all reported violations to the Post Master General of the United States, and thereto the Federal Bureau

4

of Investigations (FBI), and Secret Service having legal jurisdiction of investigation regarding violation of mail delivery laws.

On behalf of Vision Books. Thank you in advance for your support. Address any and all questions concerning this matter to Vision Books, Attn: Karl Winthers, PLLC, Attorney at Law, P.O. Box 42406, Charlotte, NC 28215-1985.

Sincerely,

Tony Rivers Sr.
Tony Rivers, Sr.
Publisher & Chief Editor

Cc: Patrick R. Donahoe, Post Master General; Gregory D. Cox, FBI-Special Agent in Charge Washington D.C. Bureau; & Guy Cottrell, Chief Postal Inspector (USPIS)

ABOUT THIS PUBLICATION

FOR SERVICE ASSISTANCE

Customer Service Department
1-980.729.3505

North Carolina General Assembly General Statues is co-published by Vision Books in Charlotte, North Carolina. Copyright 2019 by Vision Books. This book or parts thereof may not be reproduced in any form, stored in a retrieval system, or transmitted in any form by any means—electronic, mechanical, photocopy, recording or otherwise—without prior written permission of the publisher, except as provided by United States of America copyright law.

The records required by U.S. Code 2257(a) through (c) and the pertinent regulations 28 C.F.R. Cli. 1, Part 75 with respect to this publication and all materials associated with such records are maintained by USA State Code Books, LLC, Publisher and available for review by Attorney General.

www.usastatecodes.com

TID: 4985710
ISBN (10) digit: 1501077333
ISBN (13) digit: 978-1501077333

123-4-56789-09890-Paperback
123-4-56789-09891-Hardback

First Edition

111420140852

Printed in the United States of America

7

2019 EDITION

North Carolina General Assembly General Statues Reference Guide

(General Statutes of North Carolina)

Printed in conjunction with the Administration of the Courts

Chapters	Pamphlet
Chapter 1 Civil Procedure	1
Chapter 1 Civil Procedure (Continue)	2
Chapter 1A Rules of Civil Procedure	2
Chapter 1B Contribution.	2
Chapter 1C Enforcement of Judgments.	2
Chapter 1D Punitive Damages.	2
Chapter 1E Eastern Band of Cherokee Indians.	2
Chapter 1F North Carolina Uniform Interstate Depositions and Discovery Act.	2
Chapter 2 - Clerk of Superior Court [Repealed and Transferred.]	3
Chapter 3 - Commissioners of Affidavits and Deeds [Repealed.]	3
Chapter 4 - Common Law	3
Chapter 5 - Contempt [Repealed.]	3
Chapter 5A - Contempt	3
Chapter 6 - Liability for Court Costs	3
Chapter 7 - Courts [Repealed and Transferred.]	3
Chapter 7A – Judicial Department	3
Chapter 7A – Continuation (Judicial Department)	4
Chapter 7A – Continuation (Judicial Department)	5
Chapter 7B - Juvenile Code	5
Chapter 8 - Evidence	6
Chapter 8A - Interpreters for Deaf Persons [Recodified.]	6
Chapter 8B - Interpreters for Deaf Persons	6
Chapter 8C - Evidence Code	6
Chapter 9 - Jurors	6
Chapter 10 - Notaries [Repealed.]	6
Chapter 10A - Notaries [Recodified.]	6
Chapter 10B - Notaries	6
Chapter 11 - Oaths	6

Chapter 12 - Statutory Construction   6

Chapter 13 - Citizenship Restored   6

Chapter 14 - Criminal Law   7

Chapter 14 –Criminal Law (Continuation)   8

Chapter 15 - Criminal Procedure   9

Chapter 15A - Criminal Procedure Act (Continuation)   10

Chapter 15A - Criminal Procedure Act (Continuation)   11

Chapter 15B - Victims Compensation   11

Chapter 15C - Address Confidentiality Program   11

Chapter 16 - Gaming Contracts and Futures   11

Chapter 17 - Habeas Corpus   11

Chapter 17A - Law-Enforcement Officers [Recodified.]   11

Chapter 17B - North Carolina Criminal Justice   11
Education and Training System [Recodified.] Chapter 17C –
North Carolina Criminal Justice Education and Training
Standards Commission   11

Chapter 17D - North Carolina Justice Academy   11

Chapter 17E - North Carolina Sheriffs' Education and
Training Standards Commission   11

Chapter 18 - Regulation of Intoxicating Liquors [Repealed.]   12

Chapter 18A - Regulation of Intoxicating Liquors [Repealed.]   12

Chapter 18B - Regulation of Alcoholic Beverages   12

Chapter 18C - North Carolina State Lottery   12

Chapter 19 - Offenses against Public Morals   12

Chapter 19A - Protection of Animals   12

Chapter 20 - Motor Vehicles   13

Chapter 20 - Motor Vehicles (Continuation)   14

Chapter 20 - Motor Vehicles (Continuation)   15

Chapter 20 - Motor Vehicles (Continuation)   16

Chapter 21 - Bills of Lading   17

Chapter 22 - Contracts Requiring Writing   17

Chapter 22A - Signatures   17

Chapter 22B - Contracts Against Public Policy   17

Chapter 22C - Payments to Subcontractors   17

Chapter 23 - Debtor and Creditor   17

Chapter 24 – Interest   17

Chapter 25 – Uniform Commercial Code   18

Chapter 25 – Uniform Commercial Code (Continuation)   19

Chapter 25A – Retail Installment Sales Act   20

Chapter 25B - Credit   20

Chapter 25C - Sales of Artwork   20

Chapter 26 - Suretyship   20

Chapter 27 - Warehouse Receipts [Repealed.]   20

Chapter 28 - Administration [Repealed.]   20

Chapter 28A - Administration of Decedents' Estates   20

Chapter 28B - Estates of Absentees in Military Service   20

Chapter 28C - Estates of Missing Persons   20

Chapter 29 - Intestate Succession   21

Chapter 30 - Surviving Spouses   21

Chapter 31 - Wills   21

Chapter 31A - Acts Barring Property Rights   21

Chapter 31B - Renunciation of Property and Renunciation of

Fiduciary Powers Act   21

Chapter 31C - Uniform Disposition of Community Property

Rights at Death Act   21

Chapter 32 - Fiduciaries   21

Chapter 32A - Powers of Attorney   21

Chapter 33 - Guardian and Ward [Repealed and Recodified.]   21

Chapter 33A - North Carolina Uniform Transfers to Minors Act   21

Chapter 33B - North Carolina Uniform Custodial Trust Act   21

Chapter 34 - Veterans' Guardianship Act   22

Chapter 35 - Sterilization Procedures   22

12

Chapter 35A - Incompetency and Guardianship   22

Chapter 36 - Trusts and Trustees [Repealed.]   22

Chapter 36A - Trusts and Trustees   22

Chapter 36B - Uniform Management of Institutional Funds
Act [Repealed.]   22

Chapter 36C - North Carolina Uniform Trust Code   22

Chapter 36D - North Carolina Community Third Party Trusts,
Pooled Trusts   23

Chapter 36E - Uniform Prudent Management of Institutional
Funds Act   23

Chapter 37 - Allocation of Principal and Income [Repealed.]   23

Chapter 37A - Uniform Principal and Income Act   23

Chapter 38 - Boundaries   23

Chapter 38A - Landowner Liability   23

Chapter 39 - Conveyances   23

Chapter 39A - Transfer Fee Covenants Prohibited   23

Chapter 40 - Eminent Domain [Repealed.]   23

Chapter 40A - Eminent Domain   23

Chapter 41 - Estates   23

Chapter 41A - State Fair Housing Act   23

Chapter 42 - Landlord and Tenant   23

Chapter 42A - Vacation Rental Act   23

Chapter 43 - Land Registration   23

Chapter 44 - Liens   24

Chapter 44A - Statutory Liens and Charges   24

Chapter 45 - Mortgages and Deeds of Trust   24

Chapter 45A - Good Funds Settlement Act   24

Chapter 46 - Partition   24

Chapter 47 - Probate and Registration   25

Chapter 47A - Unit Ownership   25

Chapter 47B - Real Property Marketable Title Act   25

Chapter 47C - North Carolina Condominium Act   25

Chapter 47D - Notice of Settlement Act [Expired.]   25

Chapter 47E - Residential Property Disclosure Act   25

Chapter 47F - North Carolina Planned Community Act   25

Chapter 47G - Option to Purchase Contracts   25

Chapter 47H - Contracts for Deed   25

Chapter 48 - Adoptions   26

Chapter 48A - Minors   26

Chapter 49 - Bastardy   26

Chapter 49A - Rights of Children   26

Chapter 50 - Divorce and Alimony   26

Chapter 50A - Uniform Child-Custody Jurisdiction and
Enforcement Act   26

Chapter 50B - Domestic Violence   26

Chapter 50C - Civil No-Contact Orders   26

Chapter 51 - Marriage   26

Chapter 52 - Powers and Liabilities of Married Persons   27

Chapter 52A - Uniform Reciprocal Enforcement of Support
Act [Repealed.]   27

Chapter 52B - Uniform Premarital Agreement Act   27

Chapter 52C - Uniform Interstate Family Support Act   27

Chapter 53 - Banks   27

Chapter 53A - Business Development Corporations and
North Carolina Capital Resource Corporations   28

Chapter 53B - Financial Privacy Act   28

Chapter 54 - Cooperative Organizations   28

Chapter 54A - Capital Stock Savings and Loan Associations
[Repealed.]   28

Chapter 54B - Savings and Loan Associations   29

Chapter 54C - Savings Banks   29

Chapter 55 - North Carolina Business Corporation Act   30

Chapter 55A - North Carolina Nonprofit Corporation Act   31

Chapter 55B - Professional Corporation Act   31

Chapter 55C - Foreign Trade Zones   31

Chapter 55D - Filings, Names, and Registered Agents for
Corporations, Nonprofit Corporations, and Partnerships   31

Chapter 56 - Electric, Telegraph and Power Companies
[Repealed.]   31

Chapter 57 - Hospital, Medical and Dental Service
Corporations [Recodified.]   31

Chapter 57A - Health Maintenance Organization Act
[Recodified.]   31

Chapter 57B - Health Maintenance Organization Act
[Recodified.]   31

Chapter 57C - North Carolina Limited Liability Company Act.   31

Chapter 58 - Insurance.   32

Chapter 58 - Insurance (Continuation)   33

Chapter 58 - Insurance (Continuation)   34

Chapter 58 - Insurance (Continuation)   35

Chapter 58 - Insurance (Continuation)   36

Chapter 58 - Insurance (Continuation)   37

Chapter 58 - Insurance (Continuation)   38

Chapter 58A - North Carolina Health Insurance Trust
Commission [Recodified.]   38

Chapter 59 - Partnership.   39

Chapter 59B - Uniform Unincorporated Nonprofit Association Act. 39

Chapter 60 - Railroads and Other Carriers [Repealed and
Transferred.]   39

Chapter 61 - Religious Societies   39

Chapter 62 - Public Utilities   39

Chapter 62 - Public Utilities (Continuation)   40

Chapter 62A - Public Safety Telephone Service And

Wireless Telephone Service   40

Chapter 63 - Aeronautics   40

Chapter 63A - North Carolina Global Trans Park Authority   40

Chapter 64 - Aliens   40

Chapter 65 – Cemeteries   40

Chapter 66 - Commerce and Business   41

Chapter 67 - Dogs   41

Chapter 68 - Fences and Stock Law   41

Chapter 69 - Fire Protection   41

Chapter 70 - Indian Antiquities, Archaeological Resources

and Unmarked Human Skeletal Remains Protection   42

Chapter 71 - Indians [Repealed.]   42

Chapter 71A - Indians   42

Chapter 72 - Inns, Hotels and Restaurants   42

Chapter 73 - Mills   42

Chapter 74 - Mines and Quarries   42

Chapter 74A - Company Police [Repealed.]   42

Chapter 74B - Private Protective Services Act [Repealed.]   42

Chapter 74C - Private Protective Services   42

Chapter 74D - Alarm Systems   42

Chapter 74E - Company Police Act   42

Chapter 74F - Locksmith Licensing Act   42

Chapter 74G - Campus Police Act   42

Chapter 75 - Monopolies, Trusts and Consumer Protection   42

Chapter 75A - Boating and Water Safety   43

Chapter 75B - Discrimination in Business   43

Chapter 75C - Motion Picture Fair Competition Act   43

Chapter 75D - Racketeer Influenced and Corrupt Organizations   43

Chapter 75E - Unlawful Activities in Connection With

Certain Corporate Transactions   43

Chapter 76 - Navigation   43

Chapter 89E - Geologists Licensing Act   45

Chapter 89F - North Carolina Soil Scientist Licensing Act   45

Chapter 89G - Irrigation Contractors   45

Chapter 90 - Medicine and Allied Occupations   45

Chapter 90 - Medicine and Allied Occupations (Continuation)   46

Chapter 90 - Medicine and Allied Occupations (Continuation)   47

Chapter 90 - Medicine and Allied Occupations (Continuation)   48

Chapter 90A - Sanitarians and Water and Wastewater

Treatment Facility Operators   48

Chapter 90B - Social Worker Certification and Licensure Act   48

Chapter 90C - North Carolina Recreational Therapy

Licensure Act   48

Chapter 90D - Interpreters and Transliterators   48

Chapter 91 - Pawnbrokers [Repealed.]   48

Chapter 91A - Pawnbrokers Modernization Act of 1989   48

Chapter 92 - Photographers [Deleted.]   48

Chapter 93 - Certified Public Accountants   48

Chapter 93A - Real Estate License Law   49

Chapter 93B - Occupational Licensing Boards   49

Chapter 93C - Watchmakers [Repealed.]   49

Chapter 93D - North Carolina State Hearing Aid Dealers

and Fitters Board.   49

Chapter 93E - North Carolina Appraisers Act   49

Chapter 94 - Apprenticeship   49

Chapter 95 - Department of Labor and Labor Regulations   49

Chapter 95 - Department of Labor and Labor Regulations

(Continuation)   50

Chapter 96 - Employment Security   50

Chapter 97 - Workers' Compensation Act   50

Chapter 97 - Workers' Compensation Act (Continuation)   51

Chapter 98 - Burnt and Lost Records   51

18

Chapter 99 - Libel and Slander   51

Chapter 99A - Civil Remedies for Criminal Actions   51

Chapter 99B - Products Liability   51

Chapter 99C - Actions Relating to Winter Sports

Safety and Accidents   51

Chapter 99D - Civil Rights   51

Chapter 99E - Special Liability Provisions   51

Chapter 100 - Monuments, Memorials and Parks   51

Chapter 101 - Names of Persons   51

Chapter 102 - Official Survey Base   51

Chapter 103 - Sundays, Holidays and Special Days   51

Chapter 104 - United States Lands   51

Chapter 104A - Degrees of Kinship   51

Chapter 104B - Hurricanes or Other Acts of Nature   51

Chapter 104C - Atomic Energy, Radioactivity and Ionizing

Radiation [Repealed and Recodified.]   51

Chapter 104D - Southern States Energy Compact   51

Chapter 104E - North Carolina Radiation Protection Act   51

Chapter 104F - Southeast Interstate Low-Level

Radioactive Waste Management Compact [Repealed]   51

Chapter 104G - North Carolina Low-Level Radioactive

Waste Management Authority Act of 1987 [Repealed]   51

Chapter 105 - Taxation   51

Chapter 105 - Taxation (Continuation)   52

Chapter 105 - Taxation (Continuation)   53

Chapter 105 - Taxation (Continuation)   54

Chapter 105A - Setoff Debt Collection Act   55

Chapter 105B - Defaulted Student Loan Recovery Act   55

Chapter 106 - Agriculture   55

Chapter 106 - Agriculture (Continue)   56

Chapter 106 - Agriculture (Continue)   57

19

Chapter 107 - Agricultural Development Districts
[Repealed.]   57
Chapter 108 - Social Services [Repealed and Recodified.]   57
Chapter 108A - Social Services   57
Chapter 108B - Community Action Programs   58
Chapter 108C Medicaid and Health Choice
Provider Requirements.   58
Chapter 108D Medicaid Managed Care for Behavioral Health
Services.   58
Chapter 109 - Bonds [Recodified.]   58
Chapter 110 - Child Welfare   58
Chapter 111 - Aid to the Blind   58
Chapter 112 - Confederate Homes and Pensions
[Repealed.]   58
Chapter 113 - Conservation and Development   58
Chapter 113 - Conservation and Development (Continuation)   59
Chapter 113A - Pollution Control and Environment   59
Chapter 113A - Pollution Control and Environment
(Continuation)   60
Chapter 113B - North Carolina Energy Policy Act of 1975   60
Chapter 114 - Department of Justice   60
Chapter 115 - Elementary and Secondary Education
[Repealed.]   60
Chapter 115A - Community Colleges, Technical
Institutes, and Industrial Education Centers [Repealed.]   60
Chapter 115B - Tuition and Fee Waivers   60
Chapter 115C - Elementary and Secondary Education   60
Chapter 115C - Elementary and Secondary Education
(Continuation)   61
Chapter 115C - Elementary and Secondary Education
(Continuation)   62

20

Chapter 115C - Elementary and Secondary Education

(Continuation)   63

Chapter 115D - Community Colleges   63

Chapter 115E - Private Educational Facilities Finance

Act [Recodified]   63

Chapter 116 - Higher Education   63

Chapter 116 - Higher Education (Continuation)   63

Chapter 116A - Escheats and Abandoned Property

[Repealed.]   64

Chapter 116B - Escheats and Abandoned Property   64

Chapter 116C - Continuum of Education Programs   64

Chapter 116D - Higher Education Bonds   64

Chapter 116E -Education Longitudinal Data System   64

Chapter 117 - Electrification   64

Chapter 118 - Firemen's and Rescue Squad

Workers' Relief and Pension Funds [Recodified.]   64

Chapter 118A - Firemen's Death Benefit Act Repealed.]   64

Chapter 118B - Members of a Rescue Squad

Death Benefit Act [Repealed.]   64

Chapter 119 - Gasoline and Oil Inspection and Regulation   64

Chapter 120 - General Assembly   65

Chapter 120 - General Assembly (Continuation)   66

Chapter 120 - General Assembly (Continuation)   67

Chapter 120C - Lobbying   67

Chapter 121 - Archives and History   67

Chapter 122 - Hospitals for the Mentally Disordered

[Repealed.]   67

Chapter 122A - North Carolina Housing Finance Agency   67

Chapter 122B - North Carolina Agricultural Facilities

Finance Act [Repealed.]   67

Chapter 122C - Mental Health, Developmental

Disabilities, and Substance Abuse Act of 1985   67

Chapter 122C - Mental Health, Developmental

Disabilities, and Substance Abuse Act of 1985 (Continuation)   68

Chapter 122D - North Carolina Agricultural Finance Act   68

Chapter 122E - North Carolina Housing Trust and Oil

Overcharge Act   68

Chapter 123 - Impeachment   69

Chapter 123A - Industrial Development [Repealed.]   69

Chapter 124 - Internal Improvements   69

Chapter 125 - Libraries   69

Chapter 126 - State Personnel System   69

Chapter 127 - Militia [Repealed.]   69

Chapter 127A - Militia   69

Chapter 127B - Military Affairs   69

Chapter 127C - Advisory Commission on Military Affairs   69

Chapter 128 - Offices and Public Officers   69

Chapter 128 - Offices and Public Officers (Continuation)   70

Chapter 129 - Public Buildings and Grounds   70

Chapter 130 - Public Health [Repealed.]   70

Chapter 130A - Public Health   70

Chapter 130A - Public Health (Continuation)   71

Chapter 130A - Public Health (Continuation)   72

Chapter 130B - Hazardous Waste Management

Commission [Repealed.]   72

Chapter 131 - Public Hospitals [Repealed.]   72

Chapter 131A - Health Care Facilities Finance Act   72

Chapter 131B - Licensing of Ambulatory Surgical

Facilities [Repealed.]   72

Chapter 131C - Charitable Solicitation Licensure Act

[Repealed.]   72

Chapter 131D - Inspection and Licensing of Facilities   72

Chapter 131E - Health Care Facilities and Services   72

Chapter 131E - Health Care Facilities and Services
(Continuation)   73

Chapter 131F - Solicitation of Contributions   73

Chapter 132 - Public Records   73

Chapter 133 - Public Works   74

Chapter 134 - Youth Development [Recodified.]   74

Chapter 134A - Youth Services [Repealed.]   74

Chapter 135 - Retirement System for Teachers and
State Employees; Social Security; Health Insurance
Program for Children   74

Chapter 135 - Retirement System for Teachers and
State Employees; Social Security; Health Insurance
Program for Children   75

Chapter 136 - Transportation   75

Chapter 136 - Transportation (Continuation)   76

Chapter 137 - Rural Rehabilitation [Repealed.]   76

Chapter 138 - Salaries, Fees and Allowances   76

Chapter 138A - State Government Ethics Act   76

Chapter 139 - Soil and Water Conservation Districts   76

Chapter 140 - State Art Museum; Symphony and
Art Societies   76

Chapter 140A - State Awards System   76

Chapter 141 - State Boundaries   76

Chapter 142 - State Debt   76

Chapter 143 - State Departments, Institutions, and
Commissions   77

Chapter 143 - State Departments, Institutions, and
Commissions (Continuation)   78

Chapter 143 - State Departments, Institutions, and
Commissions (Continuation)   79

Chapter 143 - State Departments, Institutions, and
Commissions (Continuation)   80
Chapter 143A - State Government Reorganization   80
Chapter 143B - Executive Organization Act of 1973   80
Chapter 143B - Executive Organization Act of 1973
(Continuation)   81
Chapter 143B - Executive Organization Act of 1973
(Continuation)   82
Chapter 143C - State Budget Act   83
Chapter 143D - The State Governmental Accountability
and Internal Control Act   83
Chapter 144 - State Flag, Official Governmental Flags,
Motto, and Colors   83
Chapter 145 - State Symbols and Other Official Adoptions. 83
Chapter 146 - State Lands   83
Chapter 147 - State Officers   83
Chapter 148 - State Prison System   84
Chapter 149 - State Song and Toast   84
Chapter 150 - Uniform Revocation of Licenses
[Repealed.]   84
Chapter 150A - Administrative Procedure Act [Recodified. 84
Chapter 150B - Administrative Procedure Act   84
Chapter 151 - Constables [Repealed.]   84
Chapter 152 - Coroners   84
Chapter 152A - County Medical Examiner [Repealed.]   84
Chapter 152A - County Medical Examiner [Repealed.]
(Continuation)   85
Chapter 153 - Counties and County Commissioners
[Repealed.]   85
Chapter 153A - Counties   85
Chapter 153B - Mountain Resources Planning Act   85

Chapter 153C - Unhurried Regional Resources Act   85

Chapter 154 - County Surveyor [Repealed.]   85

Chapter 155 - County Treasurer [Repealed.]   85

Chapter 156 - Drainage   85

Chapter 156 – Drainage (Continuation)   86

Chapter 157 - Housing Authorities and Projects   86

Chapter 157A - Historic Properties Commissions [Transferred.]   86

Chapter 158 - Local Development   86

Chapter 159 - Local Government Finance   86

Chapter 159 - Local Government Finance (Continuation)   87

Chapter 159A - Pollution Abatement and Industrial

Facilities Financing Act [Unconstitutional.]   87

Chapter 159B - Joint Municipal Electric Power and

Energy Act   87

Chapter 159C - Industrial and Pollution Control

Facilities Financing Act   87

Chapter 159D - The North Carolina Capital Facilities

Financing Act   87

Chapter 159E - Registered Public Obligations Act   87

Chapter 159F - North Carolina Energy Development

Authority [Repealed.]   87

Chapter 159G - Water Infrastructure   87

Chapter 159H - [Reserved.]   87

Chapter 159I - Solid Waste Management Loan Program

and Local Government Special Obligation Bonds   87

Chapter 160 - Municipal Corporations [Repealed

And Transferred.]   87

Chapter 160A - Cities and Towns   88

Chapter 160A - Cities and Towns (Continuation)   89

Chapter 160B - Consolidated City-County Act   89

Chapter 160C - Baseball Park Districts [Repealed.]   90

25

North Carolina General Assembly
General Statues Reference Guide

Fax Orders:	1-980-299-5965
Phone Orders:	1-980-729-3505
Web Orders:	www.visionbooks.org
Mail Orders:	Vision Books P.O. Box 42406 Charlotte, NC 28215-1985

Shipp To:
Name_____
Address_____
City_____State_____Zip_____
Phone_____Fax_____
Email_____@_____

Bill To: We can bill a third party on your behalf.
Name_____
Address_____
City_____State_____Zip_____
Phone_____Fax_____
Email_____@_____

Pamphlet Number ($15.00 Each)	Qty	Total Cost
_____	_____	_____
_____	_____	_____
_____	_____	_____
_____	_____	_____
_____	_____	_____
_____	_____	_____
_____	_____	_____
Full Volume Set	92 Pamphlets	1,380.00

Free Shipping & Handling on Full Volume Orders
Add $1.00 Shipping & Handling per pamphlet $_____

Total Cost $_____

Thank you for your support. Management!

Order General Assembly General Reference Guides for other States

Fax Orders:	1-980-299-5965
Phone Orders:	1-980-729-3505
Web Orders:	www.visionbooks.org
Mail Orders:	Vision Books P.O. Box 42406 Charlotte, NC 28215-1985

Shipp To:
Name_____
Address_____
City_____State_____Zip_____
Phone_____Fax_____
Email_____@_____

Bill To: We can bill a third party on your behalf.
Name_____
_____
Address_____
_____
City_____State_____Zip

This order form is for a General Reference Guide Only. It will contain your pamphlet numbers and information on how to order your state's individual pamphlets.

Item   Qty   Total Cost

General Reference Guide for the state of:

_____   _____ $_____
Write your state name on this line.

($7.00 each General Reference Guide)

Add $1.00 Shipping & Handling per pamphlet $_____

Total Cost $_____

Thank you for your order. Management!

Did you enjoy this book?

Something you want to tell us? Please do, we'd like to hear your thoughts.

Send all written correspondence to:

Vision Books
P.O. Box 42406
Charlotte, NC 28215-1985
Email: staff@visionbooks.org

Phone Orders: 1-980-729-3505

E-mail Orders: www.visionbooks.org

Mail Orders: Vision Books
                           P.O. Box 42406
                           Charlotte, NC 28215-1985